S0-AVF-177

CANADIAN GREATS

For all the young people who are
the future of Canadian greatness.

– M.T.

Photo Credits

Page 9: House of Laura Secord, Chippawa, Ontario, 1903 (Archives of Ontario, Ministry of Education, RG 2-71, J-8. I0004205) (tinted)
Page 11: Billy Bishop Heritage Museum, Owen Sound, Ontario
Page 12: National Archives of Canada, Henry Henderson, Portrait of William A. "Billy" Bishop as a cadet at RMC in Kingston, ca. 1914, PA-203478
Page 17: National Archives of Canada, William Rider-Rider, Billy Bishop, PA-001654
Page 18: Reproduced with the permission of Veterans Affairs Canada, 2003
Page 19: Billy Bishop Heritage Museum, Owen Sound, Ontario
Page 21: B.C. Archives B-06795
Page 25: Glenbow Archives NA–1641-1 (upper); (lower) B.C. Archives E-06014 (lower)
Page 27: Glenbow Archives NA-2204-12 (upper left), NA-5395-4 (lower left), NA-1514-3 (centre), NA-273-3 (upper right), NA-2607-7 (lower right)
Page 29: Banting & Best Department of Medical Research, University of Toronto
Page 34: Banting House National Historic Site, London, Ontario
Page 35: Banting House National Historic Site, London, Ontario
Page 36: London Life-Portnoy/Hockey Hall of Fame
Page 37: Hockey Hall of Fame
Page 41: Doug MacLellan/Hockey Hall of Fame
Page 44: Dave Sandford/IIHF/Hockey Hall of Fame
Page 45: Hockey Hall of Fame (cropped and manipulated)

Page 30: Illustration by Paul Dotey

The author would like to thank Frank Smith whose insights into Billy Bishop were invaluable, and Eric Zweig for clarifying the finer points of hockey.

National Library of Canada Cataloguing in Publication

Trottier, Maxine
Canadian greats / Maxine Trottier ; illustrations by Mark Thurman.

(Scholastic Canada biographies)
ISBN 0-7791-1403-5

1. Canada--Biography--Juvenile literature. I. Thurman, Mark, 1948- II. Title. III. Series.

FC25.T76 2003   j971'.009'9   C2003-901009-0
F1005.T76 2003

ISBN-10 0-7791-1403-5 / ISBN-13 978-0-7791-1403-0

Text copyright © 2003 by Maxine Trottier.
Illustrations copyright © 2003 by Mark Thurman.
All rights reserved.

9 8 7   Printed in Canada   119   10 11 12

© **Mixed Sources**
Product group from well-managed forests, controlled sources and recycled wood or fiber
www.fsc.org Cert no. SGS-COC-003098
© 1996 Forest Stewardship Council
FSC

Scholastic Canada Biographies

CANADIAN GREATS

Maxine Trottier

illustrated by

Mark Thurman

Scholastic Canada Ltd.

Toronto New York London Auckland Sydney
Mexico City New Delhi Hong Kong Buenos Aires

Laura Secord
A Woman of Courage

Laura Ingersoll was no stranger to war. Born in Great Barrington, Massachusetts, on September 13, 1775, she spent her early childhood in the midst of the American Revolution. Her father, Thomas, became a captain, then a major, in the Massachusetts militia. The war ended in 1783, but peace did not bring happiness to Laura's life. Her mother, Elizabeth, died that same year, leaving Laura and two younger sisters.

Her father remarried in 1784, but Laura's stepmother died four years later. When he quickly remarried again, stepmother Sara came into their lives.

By 1795 there were 11 children – Laura now had four brothers and six sisters, all of whom she would help raise. Unhappy with the government's policies in the United States, her father moved the family to Upper Canada. He was given a plot of land near Queenston, not far from the Niagara River.

There, at her father's tavern, Laura met James Secord, a successful merchant and a volunteer sergeant in the 1st Lincoln Militia. They married two years later, and by 1812 had a comfortable life in their white frame house. Two servants helped with their five children. James's business selling household goods and clothing was doing well.

Then war broke out between England and the United States once more. This time Canada, a British colony, became involved. When the Americans attacked Queenston Heights that

October, Laura Secord took the children to her brother's home at St. David's. Worried about James, she returned to Queenston to learn that he had been badly hurt. She found him on the battlefield, lying among the dead and wounded, his leg shattered. Their home had been vandalized during the battle, so Laura took James to St. David's, where the children waited in safety.

That spring, in 1813, the Secords returned to Queenston. Now, though, the Americans were in control of the Canadian side of the Niagara River. Any able-bodied men had been sent to the United States as prisoners of war, but because James was still unwell, an exception was made. He remained at home.

On June 21 American officers were in the Secord home. It may be that they had demanded a meal, or perhaps they were billeted there for a while. As she served them dinner, Laura Secord overheard Colonel Boerstler tell his companions that his army would move against the British and Colonel James FitzGibbon at Beaver Dam.

Laura knew that the British must be warned, but James could not take on the task with a musket ball still lodged in his knee. It would be dangerous – wolves, bears and rattlesnakes inhabited the wild countryside. Worse, if Laura was caught, she could be shot as a spy. Still, she knew she must get word to Colonel FitzGibbon.

Laura Secord told the American officers she needed to visit her sick brother at St. David's, and she was given a pass so that she could be out after curfew.

The next day Laura set out alone, before sunrise. When she reached her brother, his young fiancée, Elizabeth, joined her.

In terrible heat they walked across the countryside and through the Black Swamp, following the creek to avoid the main roads and any American soldiers guarding them. By noon they had reached the Niagara Escarpment, but Elizabeth, exhausted, could go no further. Laura left her at a local farm.

Laura Secord went on alone. She had lost one of her shoes in the swamp, and the other as she twice crossed Ten Mile Creek. She reached the top of the escarpment, her bleeding feet bandaged with

strips she had torn from her petticoat. Unsure of where to find the house where FitzGibbon was staying, she stumbled through the woods. Then she stopped. All around her were Mohawks, the Native allies of the British. Secord convinced them to take her to FitzGibbon. Eighteen hours and 32 kilometres after she had begun her walk, Laura Secord was finally able to deliver the warning.

Two days later, FitzGibbon was ready. Fifty British soldiers and several hundred Mohawk warriors surrounded the Americans at the Battle of Beaver Dam. Colonel Boerstler and his army surrendered, and were taken as prisoners. The

Niagara Peninsula was safe.

For a long while, Laura Secord's courageous act went unrecognized. She and James filed several petitions after the war, asking for a financial reward or a job for Laura. Nothing came of them. In 1841 James died, leaving Laura a poor widow. When Albert Edward, Prince of Wales, visited Canada in 1860, Laura Secord was presented to him and he read her account of the events. Impressed, he later sent her a gift of 100 gold sovereigns.

Laura Ingersoll Secord died at the age of 93. She is buried next to her husband in Drummond Hill Cemetery, at Lundy's Lane, Ontario. Her Queenston home is now a museum – a fitting tribute to a brave Canadian.

Laura Secord's house in Chippawa, Ontario, as it appeared in 1903

Billy Bishop
The Lone Hawk

On a July day in 1915, Billy Bishop watched a biplane touch down briefly in an English field so that the pilot could get his bearings. That day was to change his life forever.

William Avery Bishop was born in Owen Sound, Ontario, on February 8, 1894. His parents, William and Margaret, knew that their son would have to work hard to do well in school. But Billy focused more on athletics and having fun. He had a natural talent for sports like riding and swimming — things he did alone. He was fearless, and this earned him the respect of his classmates.

Billy and his younger sister Louie were always very close. In high school, she persuaded him to date some of her friends. One of them was Margaret Burden, granddaughter of Timothy Eaton, the department store millionaire. Billy fell in love with her at once.

Billy as a cadet at RMC in Kingston, ca. 1914

When he was 17, his parents sent him to the Royal Military College in Kingston. Billy found the team sports and the courses tough. His older brother had been an excellent student there, and Billy was not. Bending to the discipline of the college was difficult for him. But at the end of his third year, events in the outside world cut his education short.

On July 28, 1914, Austria-Hungary declared war on Serbia. On August 3 Germany declared war on France. The next day Great Britain declared war on Germany. The First World War had begun.

Canada announced its support of Britain. Billy withdrew from the college and was commissioned into the Mississauga Horse of Toronto, a cavalry regiment of the 2nd Canadian Division. Much to his disappointment, he was in hospital with pneumonia when the Canadian Expeditionary Force left for England. It meant, though, that he was spared being part of what was to follow – the terrible losses in France of men on horseback, when they charged at trenches defended by German machine guns.

Billy Bishop was assigned to the 7th Canadian Mounted Rifles, which was being formed in London, Ontario. Before he left for England, he proposed to Margaret Burden. She accepted.

The trip across the Atlantic on the cattle ship *Caledonia* was miserable. The weather was stormy, men were

seasick and German U-boats lurked beneath the waves. Once in England, Billy Bishop began to feel that he did not want to serve on horseback. The sight of that biplane touching down in a British field convinced him to make a change. "I knew there was only one place to be on such a day – up above the clouds and in the summer sunshine. I was going into the battle that way. I was going to meet the enemy in the air."

Billy Bishop joined the Royal Flying Corps as an observer, and on January 1, 1916, his squadron was moved to France. He suffered a knee injury in a crash landing, and was returned to England where he continued to train. He received his pilot's wings there, and was promoted to captain. On March 9, 1917, he arrived at Filescamp Farm, the base of 60 Squadron in France.

The aircraft he was to fly was the single-seat Nieuport 17 Scout, a biplane much like the one he had seen two summers ago. Billy did not have the light touch necessary to fly the Nieuport, and he had a number of crash landings, one in front of several important visiting officers. On that occasion, he was told that he would need to return to England for more training.

But the next day Billy Bishop and four other pilots engaged three German aircraft. With bullets flying everywhere, Billy pursued one of the planes. As it crashed into the ground, he managed to pull his own plane out of a steep dive. Then his engine quit. Forced to glide in for a landing, less then 300 metres from the German front line trenches, Billy spent the night huddled near his aircraft.

Back at Filescamp, Billy Bishop was no longer in

any danger of being sent back to England. Instead he began a remarkable series of aerial victories. While most pilots were assigned to missions for a number of days, Billy continued to fly planes into the heart of danger for months. By the age of 23, Billy Bishop was a flying ace – a man they called "The Lone Hawk" because he preferred solo missions.

Billy Bishop in a Nieuport aircraft of the Royal Flying Corps

Medals came one after the other, from Britain and France. In June of 1917 he was awarded the Distinguished Service Order "for conspicuous gallantry and devotion to duty. While in a single

The Distinguished
Service Order

The Victoria Cross

seater, he attacked three hostile machines, two of which he brought down, although in the meantime he was himself attacked by four other hostile machines. His courage and determination have set a fine example to others." Two months later, he received the Victoria Cross "for most conspicuous bravery, determination and skill," for a mission in which he single-handedly flew against a German aerodrome.

Due to concern that such an outstanding pilot would be killed – he had shot down 72 enemy planes and survived an encounter with Germany's most feared pilot, the Red Baron – he was finally withdrawn from active duty in 1918. That same year he published his war memoirs, *Winged Warfare*.

In 1928 Billy Bishop was the guest of honour at a gathering of German air aces in Berlin. Even though he had been a fearsome enemy, he was made an honorary member of their association in recognition of his daring. During the Second World War, Bishop went on to serve as the Director of Recruiting for the Royal Canadian Air Force.

Billy Bishop died on September 11, 1956. He had shown a rare sort of bravery in battle, what his son referred to as "the courage of the early morning." He was a true Canadian hero of the skies.

Billy's boyhood home in Owen Sound,
now The Billy Bishop Heritage Museum

Nellie McClung
The Change Maker

Nellie Mooney was born near Chatsworth, Ontario, on October 20, 1873. The youngest of six children, she was seven years old when her family decided to sell their farm and begin homesteading at Souris Valley, Manitoba. Nellie was independent and spirited. Once, looking forward to a town picnic, she hoped there would be a race for the girls. There was not. The girls' long skirts might fly up, and they were not allowed to show their ankles and legs. "I wanted to know why," she later wrote, "but I was hushed up."

Busy helping on the farm, Nellie did not attend school until she was 10 years old. But that did not dampen her love of learning. She developed strong opinions about politics and the world. From an early age, she showed that fairness was very important to her.

In 1889, wanting to be a teacher, she went to Winnipeg to enroll in a five-month training programme. Nellie received her teaching certificate, and was teaching all eight grades in a one-room schoolhouse when she was 16. She would sometimes play football with the students at recess. Parents did not approve of this at first, but in time she won them over. The next year she was teaching in Manitou, and boarding with the Reverend James McClung and his wife, Annie. Annie McClung had a great influence on Nellie. She introduced her to the Women's Christian Temperance Union, an organization of women concerned about the problems that alcohol could cause to families. Nellie came to share their view that all use of alcohol should be avoided.

One other person in the McClung household – Annie's son, a pharmacist called Wesley – had a

deep effect on Nellie. She married him in 1896, after a five-year courtship, and gave up her teaching.

Other careers were waiting for her, though. She became the mother of five children. And she wrote. In 1908, the first of her 16 successful books, *Sowing Seeds in Danny*, was published. It was a Canadian best-seller for a long time. She became a gifted public speaker and a politician.

But she is best remembered for her work in women's rights.

Nellie McClung and her family moved to Winnipeg in 1911, and there she became what was called a suffragist. Deeply religious and devoted to her own husband and children, she had seen firsthand the difficult lives of women and children. Many of them lived with poverty, overwork and alcohol abuse. "The real spirit of the suffrage movement," she wrote, "is sympathy and interest in the other woman, and the desire to make the world a more homelike place to live in."

Many women endured difficult lives of poverty and overwork.

Nellie McClung started to give readings from her books. Then she began to lecture, entertaining her listeners as she spoke on temperance and women's rights. By the time she and her family moved to Alberta in 1914, she had become a champion of women's

O. I. SAY
TOWN HALL
To-Night
JULY 7th   8 p. m.

Will be the scene of the greatest rally to hear

NELLIE McCLUNG
ever experienced in Macleod

She is acknowledged Canadas greatest entertainer and oratoress and will be heard in her best form on the much discussed **Drink Question**

You can't afford to miss hearing
NELLIE McCLUNG
COME EARLY AND SECURE A SEAT

Advertisement for a public speech in Fort Macleod, Alberta

suffrage. Knowing that women could influence the liquor trade if they could vote, she and other suffragists set out to win this right for women. In

1916, thanks to their work, Alberta women — as well as women in Saskatchewan and Manitoba — won the right to vote and to run for public office. British Columbia followed in 1917. Things were beginning to change.

On July 18, 1921, Nellie McClung was elected to the Alberta legislature. Only two women before her had served in a Canadian provincial government. Her work for women's rights continued.

By 1928, women could vote in all provinces but Quebec. But they still could not be appointed to the Senate, on the grounds that a woman was not a "person." A woman wasn't a person? Nellie McClung disagreed. She banded together with four other women — they came to be called the Famous Five — to ask the Supreme Court of Canada to explain the law. When the court ruled that "person" did not include "female persons," the Famous Five were not pleased. They took what came to be known as the Persons Case all the way to Canada's highest court of appeal, in London, England. There, on October 18, 1929, the British Privy Council ruled that women were persons under the law. They could indeed serve as members of the Senate in Canada.

Irene Parlby   Emily Murphy
Nellie McClung

Louise McKinney
Henrietta Muir Edwards

The Famous Five

An important victory had been won for women across Canada – one that was not popular with everyone at the time. McClung, though, believing firmly in what had been accomplished, later said, "Never retreat, never explain, never apologize – get the thing done and let them howl."

Nellie McClung died at her home in Victoria, British Columbia, on September 1, 1951. The headstone on her grave reads "Loved and Remembered." Her name lives on – a powerful Canadian symbol of women's struggle for equal rights and a better life.

Sir Frederick Banting
A Hero of Science

In 1922, 14-year-old Leonard Thompson lay dying in Toronto from a disease called diabetes. No one really understood this disease. Scientists still had not been able to unlock its mysteries. Leonard did not yet know he would be part of an experiment that would change the world, and that Dr. Frederick Banting would be responsible.

Frederick was born at his parents' farm in Alliston, Ontario, on November 14, 1891, the last of six children. He did not always want to be a doctor. At first he studied to be a minister, and then switched to medicine. The First World War broke out while he was at university, and by 1916 he was accepted into the Canadian Army Medical Corps. Two years later he was wounded at the battle of Cambrai in France, and in 1919 he was awarded the Military Cross for heroism under fire.

After the war ended, Dr. Banting returned to Canada. He began to practise medicine in London, Ontario. It was there, after reading an article about an organ called the pancreas, that an idea came to him.

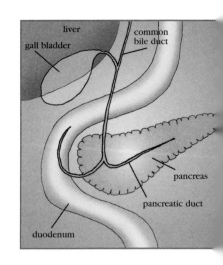

Scientists knew that diabetes was somehow connected to the pancreas. A healthy pancreas seemed to produce a substance that helped the body use sugar. A diseased pancreas did not, and so sugar would build up in the body, causing diabetes. It always ended in death. If that substance could be collected and injected into the bloodstreams of diabetic people, then perhaps the disease could be treated.

But how to collect the substance? Dr. Banting

asked himself. If you tied off the pancreatic duct —
a vein-like tube — you could isolate the pancreas,
and the substance would be trapped inside. It just
might work.

Dr. Banting took his idea to Professor John
Macleod, a respected physiologist who worked
at the University of Toronto. Macleod could see
the value of the study that Banting was proposing.
When Macleod left on vacation in the summer
of 1921, he provided Banting with a laboratory
and a research assistant, a medical student called
Charles Best.

The medical experiments could not be performed
on human beings.
But all mammals
have a pancreas, so
the study went
forward using test
animals — dogs that
were housed in the
laboratory's well-
kept kennel. In
surgery, Dr. Banting
tied off the duct of

a dog's pancreas. The pancreas shrank, and in a second surgery, Banting removed the shrunken organ. With no pancreas, the dog was diabetic. Banting ground up the pancreas, added a saline solution, strained the mixture and injected it into the dog. When Best tested the dog's urine and blood for sugar, they saw that the injection had worked. One dog, named Marjorie, was kept alive for 70 days with injections.

Neither man was being paid. They scrounged meals. Banting sold his car and borrowed money from his brothers and father. But the two men were determined to continue with their research.

When Macleod returned from vacation that September, he was impressed. However, more experiments were necessary before the substance could be used on humans, and they needed to find a source for it. It was Dr. Banting's idea to take the pancreases from the bodies of unborn calves. A biochemist, Dr. James Collip, was asked to help Macleod purify the substance. They called it insulin. To be cautious, Banting and Best tested the insulin by injecting it into each other.

On January 23, 1922, Dr. Frederick Banting injected two doses of the "thick brown muck" into a human being for the very first time. It was teenager Leonard Thompson, a charity patient at Toronto General Hospital. At this point, he weighed only 29 kilograms, and was close to death. The results were disappointing. Then Leonard was injected with some of Collip's refined insulin, and the results were immediate. Leonard's blood sugar levels dropped, and he began to gain weight. Banting knew that diabetes could now be controlled.

That March there was a front-page banner headline in the *Toronto Daily Star.* "Toronto Doctors on Track of Diabetes Cure," it read. So great were the pleas for insulin that it was not until the next year that the supply could keep up with the demand.

The Nobel Medal for Physiology or Medicine

On February 26, 1923, the Nobel Prize in medicine was awarded to Banting and Macleod. Banting felt that the credit given Macleod, who had not participated in the discovery, was unfair, so he shared his half of the prize money with Best. Macleod divided his share with Collip.

In 1934 Banting was knighted for his remarkable discovery, which was saving the lives of countless diabetics around the world.

When the Second World War broke out, Sir Frederick Banting served as a liaison officer between the British and North American medical services. But on February 21, 1941, he was killed when the plane taking him to England crashed in Newfoundland. His grave is not far from that of Charles Best in Toronto's Mount Pleasant Cemetery.

Banting House in London, where Frederick Banting first dreamed of a cure for diabetes, is a National Historic Site. Outside it stands a cairn upon which burns the Flame of Hope.

Banting's outstanding work gave the world a treatment for this deadly disease. On the day that a cure for diabetes is discovered, the flame will be extinguished. With that hope, diabetes research continues.

The Flame of Hope

Wayne at seven years old

Wayne Gretzky
The Great One

Brantford, Ontario, is a city like any other in Canada, but it has something no other community has. Beneath the sign that marks Brantford's city limits is a simple sign that reads, "Home of Wayne Gretzky."

Wayne was born on January 26, 1961, the first child of Walter and Phyllis Gretzky. Before long he was sharing the house on Varadi Avenue, where his parents still live, with his brothers Keith, Brent and Glen, and his sister Kim. Wayne's parents believed that sports were important, and that playing sports helped kids to mature and to work for what they wanted.

Almost from the beginning, hockey was a part of Wayne's life.

"Hockey Night in Canada" was a Saturday evening ritual in his grandparents' house. Wayne would slide around the floor in front of the TV in his stocking feet, batting around a rubber ball with a miniature hockey stick, his grandmother in a chair, playing goalie. When he was two years old, his mother bought him his first pair of skates. That winter he learned to skate on the Nith River below his grandparents' farm, the same way other kids had – falling and getting up and falling again.

Soon, Wayne's father began building a big ice rink in the backyard every winter. He had become tired of freezing in the car while Wayne played hockey at the park long after the other kids had gone home. He nicknamed the rink "Wally's Coliseum."

When Wayne was six, he began playing organized hockey with 10-year-olds on the Brantford major novice team, scoring his first goal during the 1967-68 season. He was so small that when the other players surrounded him to congratulate him, he disappeared.

At 16, Wayne was far from home playing junior hockey for the Sault Ste. Marie Greyhounds.

He scored 70 goals and earned 112 assists in 64 games. Number 99 was on his back for the first time — on its way to becoming the biggest number in hockey history.

The next fall Wayne began his professional career with the Indianapolis Racers. He was traded to the Edmonton Oilers that same season. There he spent 10 years demonstrating his amazing abilities and leading the Oilers to four Stanley Cup championships: in 1984, 1985, 1987 and 1988. Then his career took a startling turn. Canada's hockey hero was traded to the Los Angeles Kings. He went on to play for the St. Louis Blues and the New York Rangers.

Wayne Gretzky won the Hart Trophy as the National Hockey League's most valuable player every year from 1980 to 1987, and again in 1989. He earned the Art Ross

Gretzky receiving the Art Ross Trophy, 1990

Trophy as the league's leader 10 times — every year from 1981 to 1987, and in 1990, 1991 and 1994. To this day, he has scored more NHL goals — 894 — than anyone else, surpassing his boyhood hero, Gordie Howe, who scored 801.

The area behind the net became known as "Wayne's office" because he used it so often to set up goals

It was during his time with the Edmonton Oilers that Wayne Gretzky earned the name The Great One. He possessed exceptional skills, but there was more to it than that. He was a true team player, and is still the reigning king of assists – with a towering total of 1,963 in regular season play.

Along with the four Stanley Cup rings he won with the Oilers, Wayne Gretzky's honours include five Lester B. Pearson Awards (voted Most Valuable Player of the league by the players) and five Lady Byng Trophies (as the league's most gentlemanly player), plus many trophies and awards from All-Star games and international tournaments.

Gretzky was a player with real style and imagination. One night, during an Oilers game against the St. Louis Blues, he scored from behind the net. He had flipped the puck off the back of goalie Mike Liut. The same night, he scored directly from a face-off – twice.

Wayne's father Walter always told him, "Go to where the puck is going, not to where it has been." He was talking about hockey, but he could have been talking about life. Look forward, not back. Wayne Gretzky did just that. He played his last game with the New York Rangers and skated off the ice at 4:15 p.m., April 18, 1999. The Great One had retired, and so had number 99.

The Hockey Hall of Fame in Toronto waived its usual three-year waiting period. Seven months later, with his family proudly watching the ceremony, Wayne Gretzky was inducted into the Hall of Fame. A huge exhibit there includes all of the memorabilia his father saved over the years. "We have everything but his pacifier," declared one of the Hall's officials.

In 2002 the Canadian men's hockey team went

Wayne Gretzky in the gold medal dressing room in Salt Lake City, presenting the loonie to Phil Pritchard, Curator at the Hockey Hall of Fame

to the Winter Olympics in Salt Lake City and won a gold medal. Wayne Gretzky was the inspirational Executive Director. After the win he asked for the loonie that the icemaker had embedded beneath centre ice, so that it could go on display at the Hall of Fame.

Wayne Gretzky's influence continues to be felt. His greatness is not just about being one of the best hockey players ever. It is also about how he saw the game. Gretzky consistently played hockey like a gentleman, never resorting to violence. He once said, "I studied the game. I respected everyone I ever played against. And I was ready to play every night." Today, helping people through the work he does with many charities, he is a hockey humanitarian, and still The Great One.

Wayne's first pair of skates